THIS JOURNAL BELONGS TO:

____

____

REV DR.
Marcia Neveu

MARCIANEVEU.COM

ALL RIGHTS RESERVED

Hello! My name is Marcia, though many know me more fondly as Ama. Over the years, I've faced a variety of challenges that have shaped my journey. From battling health issues and anxiety to grappling with my identity, experiencing grief, and struggling with a lack of confidence, I've encountered many obstacles. Along the way, I've also learned the critical importance of self-care and taking time to nurture myself.

These experiences, though difficult, have taught me invaluable lessons and helped me grow into a better, more resilient version of myself. I've come to understand that while life's struggles can be overwhelming, they also offer opportunities for profound personal growth and transformation.

Through this series of journals, I want to share the insights and wisdom I've gained from my journey. My hope is that these reflections and lessons will resonate with you and provide guidance, support, and inspiration as you navigate your own path. Whether you're facing similar challenges or simply seeking encouragement, I believe these journals can offer something meaningful and helpful.

Thank you for joining me on this journey. I hope my experiences and learnings will be as beneficial to you as they have been to me.

ALL RIGHTS RESERVED

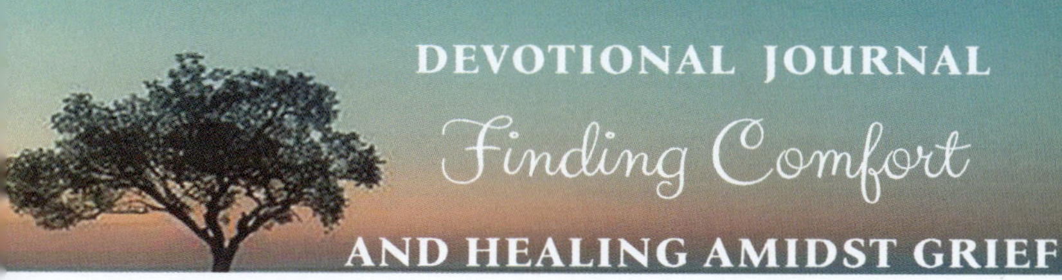

Psalm 147:3
"He healeth the broken in heart, and bindeth up their wounds."

MARCIANEVEU.COM

ALL RIGHTS RESERVED

Finding Comfort and Healing in the Midst of Grief - Devotional Journal
Marcia E Neveu
Birmingham, UK
www.marcianeveu.com
ISBN: 978-1-905028-91-7
Copyright © 2024 Marcia E Neveu
Publisher: Marcia E Neveu
Birmingham UK

All rights reserved. No part of this publication may be reproduced, stored in a retrieval system or transmitted in any form or by any means, electronic, mechanical, photocopying, recording or otherwise – except for brief quotations in printed reviews, without the prior permission in writing from the publisher.

Welcome to "Finding Comfort - And Healing Amidst Grief." In the midst of life's trials and tribulations, grief can often feel like an insurmountable burden. The loss of a loved one, the shattering of dreams, or the pain of separation can leave us feeling adrift and alone. Yet, within the pages of this journal lies a beacon of hope, a sanctuary of solace, and a pathway to healing deeply rooted in Christian faith.

Grief is a universal experience that touches every soul, but the journey through it is uniquely personal. This journal is designed to be a faithful companion on your path, offering a space where you can pour out your heart, reflect on your journey, and find the strength to move forward. It is a testament to the enduring promise of God's love and the transformative power of faith.

Within these pages, you will find:

Guided Reflections: Thought-provoking prompts that encourage you to explore your emotions, memories, and thoughts, helping you to process your grief in a healthy and constructive way. *Prayers* that offer comfort and strength, inviting you to lean into your faith and seek solace in God's presence.
Scripture passages from the Bible that provide wisdom, encouragement, and hope, reminding you of God's unwavering love and the promise of eternal life.
Personal Growth Exercises: Activities that promote healing, self-discovery, and spiritual resilience, helping you to rebuild your life and find joy amidst sorrow.

 ALL RIGHTS RESERVED

This journal is more than just a collection of words; it is a lifeline to hold onto when the waves of grief threaten to overwhelm you. It is a reminder that you are not alone, that God is with you every step of the way, and that there is hope and healing to be found even in the darkest of times.

As you embark on this journey, may you find solace in the presence of the Almighty, strength in the embrace of community, and renewal in the promise of a brighter tomorrow. Take your time with these pages; let them be a refuge where you can rest, reflect, and rejuvenate. Allow the gentle guidance of this journal to lead you towards a place of peace, restoration, and wholeness.

May this journal serve as a beacon of light amidst the shadows, guiding you through the valleys of grief towards the mountaintops of hope. May you find comfort in God's unfailing love, and may you discover the healing that flows from His grace. In these pages, may you find the **courage** to grieve, the **faith** to believe, and the **strength** to heal.

May you find comfort, and may you find healing, amidst grief

 ALL RIGHTS RESERVED

 ALL RIGHTS RESERVED

Day 1: Finding Comfort in God's Presence

Psalm 34:18 (KJV) "The LORD is nigh unto them that are of a broken heart; and saveth such as be of a contrite spirit."

During the depths of grief, it may seem as though you are utterly alone, but take solace in the knowledge that the Lord is near, especially to those with broken hearts. He understands your pain intimately and is there to offer His comforting presence. When grief threatens to overwhelm you, turn to Him. Spend time in His presence, pour out your heart in prayer, and allow His love to envelop you like a warm embrace. Today, reflect on the moments when you have felt God's closeness during your journey of grief. *How has His presence provided comfort and strength? How can you draw closer to God in times of sorrow?*

 ALL RIGHTS RESERVED

 ALL RIGHTS RESERVED

DAY 2: FINDING HOPE IN THE PROMISE OF ETERNAL LIFE

1 Corinthians 15:22 (KJV) "For as in Adam all die, even so in Christ shall all be made alive."

Grief often feels like an endless night, but through Christ, there is a dawn of hope awaiting you. In Him, we find the promise of eternal life. Remember that your loved one who has passed away is now in the arms of the Savior, experiencing a joy beyond imagination. As you grieve, hold fast to the hope of reunion in eternity. Reflect on the impact your loved one had on your life and the legacy they left behind. How can you honor their memory by spreading love and hope to others?

How does the promise of eternal life in Christ bring you hope during your grieving process?

 ALL RIGHTS RESERVED

 ALL RIGHTS RESERVED

Day 3: Finding Healing Through God's Word

Psalm 119:105 (KJV) "Thy word is a lamp unto my feet, and a light unto my path."

During times of grief, the Bible becomes a source of guidance and healing. God's Word serves as a comforting presence, illuminating the path through the darkness of sorrow. Take solace in the wisdom and comfort found in Scripture. As you read and meditate on His Word, allow it to bring healing to your wounded heart. Reflect on how the verses you've read have provided you with direction and solace during your journey through grief.

How can you incorporate God's Word more deeply into your daily life for continued healing? How has God's Word provided guidance and comfort during your grief? Is there a particular verse or passage that has been especially meaningful to you during this time of sorrow?

 ALL RIGHTS RESERVED

ALL RIGHTS RESERVED

Day 4: Finding Strength in God's Promises

Isaiah 41:10 (KJV) "Fear thou not; for I am with thee: be not dismayed; for I am thy God: I will strengthen thee; yea, I will help thee; yea, I will uphold thee with the right hand of my righteousness."

In moments of grief, fear can be overwhelming, but God offers His promise of strength and support. He reassures us not to be afraid, for He is with us. Take time today to reflect on the times when you felt God's strength upholding you during difficult moments of grief. *How has His promise to strengthen, help, and uphold you with His righteousness been a source of comfort and courage? How can you lean on God's promises for strength in times of fear and sorrow?*

 ALL RIGHTS RESERVED

 ALL RIGHTS RESERVED

DAY 5: FINDING PEACE THROUGH PRAYER

Philippians 4:6-7 (KJV) "Be careful for nothing; but in every thing by prayer and supplication with thanksgiving let your requests be made known unto God. And the peace of God, which passeth all understanding, shall keep your hearts and minds through Christ Jesus."

In the midst of grief, it's natural to be filled with cares and worries. However, the Lord invites you to bring your burdens to Him through prayer. As you pour out your heart in supplication, remember to also offer thanksgiving for the memories and blessings you shared with your loved one. In return, God promises a peace that surpasses understanding, guarding your heart and mind. Take time today to reflect on the power of prayer in finding peace amidst grief.

How has God's peace sustained you during times of uncertainty? In what ways can you cultivate a habit of prayer and thanksgiving in your life to experience God's peace more fully?

 ALL RIGHTS RESERVED

 ALL RIGHTS RESERVED

Day 6: Finding Purpose in Serving Others

Galatians 6:2 (KJV) "Bear ye one another's burdens, and so fulfil the law of Christ."

Grief can sometimes make you feel isolated, but God calls us to bear one another's burdens. By reaching out to help and support others who are also grieving, you not only fulfill the law of Christ but also find purpose in your own journey. Even though you're hurting today, reflect on how you can be a source of comfort and encouragement to someone else who is grieving today. In doing so, you may discover healing for your own heart as well.

Is there a specific person you know who could benefit from your support and encouragement today?

 ALL RIGHTS RESERVED

ALL RIGHTS RESERVED

Day 7: Finding Joy in God's Presence

Psalm 16:11 (KJV) "Thou wilt shew me the path of life: in thy presence is fulness of joy; at thy right hand there are pleasures for evermore."

Even in the midst of grief, there is a path to joy through God's presence. As you seek Him daily, you'll find that His presence holds the fullness of joy. Take time to reflect on moments when you've experienced joy in God's presence during your grieving journey. How can you cultivate a sense of joy in your life, even as you navigate the pain of loss? When have you felt the presence of God bringing joy into your grieving heart?

 ALL RIGHTS RESERVED

ALL RIGHTS RESERVED

DAY 8: FINDING REST IN GOD'S COMFORT

Matthew 11:28-29 (KJV) "Come unto me, all ye that labour and are heavy laden, and I will give you rest. Take my yoke upon you, and learn of me; for I am meek and lowly in heart: and ye shall find rest unto your souls."

Grief can be exhausting, but Jesus offers rest for your weary soul. He invites you to come to Him and find comfort. Today, reflect on the times when you've found rest in God's comforting embrace. How can you continue to seek His rest and learn from Him as you journey through grief? When have you experienced rest in God's comforting presence during your grief?

 ALL RIGHTS RESERVED

ALL RIGHTS RESERVED

Day 9: God's Tender Healing

Psalm 147:3 - "He heals the brokenhearted and binds up their wounds."

Today, as you embark on this journey of healing from grief, remember that God is close to the brokenhearted. Just as a skilled physician carefully tends to wounds, our Heavenly Father is here to mend the broken pieces of your heart. Take a moment to reflect on the wounds caused by your grief. What specific areas of your heart need His healing touch? How has your grief affected you physically, emotionally, and spiritually?

In what ways have you seen God's healing touch in your life before? How can you lean on those experiences now? Pour out your pain to Him, trusting that He is ever ready to bring solace and restoration to your soul.

 ALL RIGHTS RESERVED

 ALL RIGHTS RESERVED

Day 10: Finding Hope in God's Plan

Jeremiah 29:11 (KJV) "For I know the thoughts that I think toward you, saith the LORD, thoughts of peace, and not of evil, to give you an expected end."

Grief can leave you questioning the future, but God assures us of His good plans for our lives. Even in the midst of sorrow, He has thoughts of peace and a hopeful future for you. Reflect on how you've seen God's plans unfold in your life, even during times of grief.

How can you trust in His sovereignty and find hope in His promises today? How have you seen God's plans for your life unfold, even in times of grief?

 ALL RIGHTS RESERVED

ALL RIGHTS RESERVED

Day 11: Finding Comfort in God's Love

Romans 8:38-39 (KJV) "For I am persuaded, that neither death, nor life, nor angels, nor principalities, nor powers, nor things present, nor things to come, Nor height, nor depth, nor any other creature, shall be able to separate us from the love of God, which is in Christ Jesus our Lord."

Grief can make you feel alone and disconnected, but God's love is unwavering and unbreakable. Reflect on the unending love of God, which transcends all circumstances and trials.
How has this love been a source of comfort and reassurance in your journey through grief? In what ways can you remind yourself daily of God's constant love for you? Today, meditate on the depth of God's love and how it continues to hold you close.

 ALL RIGHTS RESERVED

ALL RIGHTS RESERVED

Day 12: Finding Peace Through Forgiveness

Colossians 3:13 (KJV) "Forbearing one another, and forgiving one another, if any man have a quarrel against any: even as Christ forgave you, so also do ye."

Grief can sometimes be accompanied by feelings of anger or resentment. Yet, God calls us to forgive as Christ forgave us. Reflect on any unresolved conflicts or feelings you may have. How can forgiveness bring you inner peace and release the burden of bitterness?
Are there any unresolved conflicts or unforgiveness in your heart related to your grief? Is there someone you need to forgive or seek forgiveness from today? Today, consider the power of forgiveness and how it can contribute to your healing process.

 ALL RIGHTS RESERVED

 ALL RIGHTS RESERVED

DAY 13: FINDING COMFORT IN COMMUNITY

Ecclesiastes 4:9-10 (KJV) "Two are better than one; because they have a good reward for their labour. For if they fall, the one will lift up his fellow: but woe to him that is alone when he falleth; for he hath not another to help him up."

God designed us to find comfort in the company of others - especially other believers. Reflect on the importance of community and the support you've received from friends and loved ones during your grieving journey.
How can you lean on your community for strength and support, and in turn, offer your support to those in need? Today, consider the significance of bearing one another's burdens in times of sorrow.

 ALL RIGHTS RESERVED

 ALL RIGHTS RESERVED

Day 14: Finding Renewal in God's Mercies

Lamentations 3:22-23 (KJV) "It is of the LORD'S mercies that we are not consumed, because his compassions fail not. They are new every morning: great is thy faithfulness."

Grief can be overwhelming, but God's mercies are new every morning. Reflect on the faithfulness of God and how His compassion sustains you day by day. *How have you witnessed His faithfulness in the midst of sorrow? In what ways can you remind yourself of His faithfulness each day, especially in times of sorrow?* Today, meditate on the promise of His unwavering love and the renewal it brings to your spirit.

 ALL RIGHTS RESERVED

 ALL RIGHTS RESERVED

Day 15: Finding Strength in Praise

Psalm 42:11 (KJV) "Why art thou cast down, O my soul? and why art thou disquieted within me? hope thou in God: for I shall yet praise him, who is the health of my countenance, and my God."

During times of grief, it's natural to feel depressed (even King David felt this way), but God invites you to place your hope in Him and find strength in praise. Reflect on moments when you've praised God despite your circumstances and how it lifted your spirits. *In what ways can you incorporate praise and worship into your daily life?* Today, consider how praising God can be a source of healing and renewal for your soul.

 ALL RIGHTS RESERVED

 ALL RIGHTS RESERVED

Day 16: Finding Strength in God's Word

Psalm 119:50 (KJV) "This is my comfort in my affliction: for thy word hath quickened me."

During times of affliction and grief, God's Word becomes a source of comfort and strength. Reflect on how His Word has breathed life into your weary soul during difficult moments. How can you continue to seek solace and renewal through reading and meditating on the Scriptures? Write down top scriptures that you find comfort in and think about how these words have brought your comfort.
In what ways can you make reading and meditating on Scripture a regular part of your life for ongoing comfort and renewal?

 ALL RIGHTS RESERVED

ALL RIGHTS RESERVED

DAY 17: FINDING STRENGTH IN GOD'S SOVEREIGNTY

Isaiah 40:28-31 (KJV) "Hast thou not known? hast thou not heard, that the everlasting God, the LORD, the Creator of the ends of the earth, fainteth not, neither is weary? there is no searching of his understanding. He giveth power to the faint; and to them that have no might he increaseth strength. Even the youths shall faint and be weary, and the young men shall utterly fall: But they that wait upon the LORD shall renew their strength; they shall mount up with wings as eagles; they shall run, and not be weary; and they shall walk, and not faint."

Grief can be physically and emotionally draining, but God promises to renew the strength of those who wait upon Him. Reflect on the unending strength and sovereignty of God.
How have you experienced His renewing power during times of weakness? Today, meditate on the assurance that those who trust in the Lord will find their strength renewed, allowing them to rise above life's challenges.

 ALL RIGHTS RESERVED

 ALL RIGHTS RESERVED

Day 18: Finding Peace Through Trust

Proverbs 3:5-6 (KJV) "Trust in the LORD with all thine heart; and lean not unto thine own understanding. In all thy ways acknowledge him, and he shall direct thy paths."

Grief often brings confusion and questions, but God calls us to trust in Him completely. Reflect on the times when you've placed your trust in the Lord and witnessed His guidance. Today, meditate on the peace that comes from trusting God to direct your paths.
How can you surrender your understanding and acknowledge Him in all aspects of your life, especially during the grieving process? When have you experienced peace through trusting in the Lord's guidance during your grief?

 ALL RIGHTS RESERVED

 ALL RIGHTS RESERVED

DAY 19: FINDING HEALING IN GOD'S TIMING

Ecclesiastes 3:1, 4 (KJV) "To every thing there is a season, and a time to every purpose under the heaven... A time to weep, and a time to laugh; a time to mourn, and a time to dance."

Grief has its own timing, but God reminds us that there is a season and a purpose for everything under heaven. Reflect on the ebb and flow of life's seasons and how they apply to your journey through grief.

How can you find comfort in knowing that mourning is part of life's rhythm, and there will be a time for joy and laughter once more? How have you experienced the ebb and flow of life's seasons in your grief journey?

 ALL RIGHTS RESERVED

ALL RIGHTS RESERVED

Day 20: Finding Hope in God's Light

Psalm 27:1 (KJV) "The LORD is my light and my salvation; whom shall I fear? the LORD is the strength of my life; of whom shall I be afraid?"

In the darkness of grief, God is your guiding light and your source of hope. Reflect on the ways in which God's light has illuminated your path during times of sorrow. Today, meditate on the assurance that you need not fear when the Lord is your light. Think about how God is light and in Him is no darkness at all (1 John 1:5).
How can you trust Him as your salvation and strength in the midst of fear and uncertainty? How has God showed up and guided you through the darkness of grief and provided hope?

 ALL RIGHTS RESERVED

 ALL RIGHTS RESERVED

Day 21: Finding Comfort in God's Peace

John 14:27 (KJV) "Peace I leave with you, my peace I give unto you: not as the world giveth, give I unto you. Let not your heart be troubled, neither let it be afraid."

Grief can bring turmoil to your heart, but Jesus offers a peace that transcends the world's understanding. Reflect on the gift of His peace and how it has calmed your troubled heart. Today, meditate on the comfort of Jesus' promise of peace.

How can you actively seek this peace in the midst of grief and trust that your heart need not be afraid? How has Jesus' peace brought comfort to your heart during your grief journey?

 ALL RIGHTS RESERVED

ALL RIGHTS RESERVED

1. Psalm 34:18 NASB - The Lord is near to the brokenhearted and saves those who are crushed in spirit.

2. Matthew 5:4 NIV - Blessed are those who mourn, for they will be comforted.

3. Isaiah 53:4 NKJV - Jesus Wants to Carry Your Pain - Surely He has borne our griefs and carried our sorrows.

4. John 14:27 NLT - Peace I leave with you; my peace I give to you. Not as the world gives do I give to you. Let not your hearts be troubled, neither let them be afraid.

5. Philippians 2:20 NIV - I have no one else like him, who will show genuine concern for your welfare.

6. 1 Thessalonians 4:13-14 NIV - Brothers and sisters, we do not want you to be uninformed about those who sleep in death, so that you do not grieve like the rest of mankind, who have no hope. For we believe that Jesus died and rose again, and so we believe that God will bring with Jesus those who have fallen asleep in him.

7. Joshua 1:9 NIV - Have I not commanded you? Be strong and courageous. Do not be afraid; do not be discouraged, for the LORD your God will be with you wherever you go.

8. Psalm 147:3 NIV - He heals the brokenhearted and binds up their wounds.

9. Psalm 34:18 NIV - The LORD is close to the brokenhearted and saves those who are crushed in spirit.

10. Revelation 21:4 NIV - He will wipe every tear from their eyes. There will be no more death' or mourning or crying or pain, for the old order of things has passed away.

 ALL RIGHTS RESERVED

Printed in Great Britain
by Amazon